English
10 Minute Tests
9–10 years

Test 1: **Mixed**

Add the missing commas to these sentences.

1–2 On her way to school Carys realised she had forgotten her glasses swimming things reading book and recorder.

3–4 Dave and Tim struggled through the rain slipping on rocks and stumbling through the mud as they hurried to reach cover.

Complete the word sums. Watch out for the spelling changes!

5   depend + able   _____   8   doubt + ful   _____

6   early + er   _____   9   likely + hood   _____

7   cord + less   _____   10   response + ible   _____

Give one word for each of these *definitions*. Each word begins with the letter p.

11   A code of letters and numbers at the end of an address to help with the sorting and delivering of mail.

_____

12   A coin.

_____

13   A drawing or painting of someone, usually showing their head and shoulders.

_____

14   A male member of a royal family.

_____

15   The sweet part of a meal.

_____

Write the following *adjectives* of comparison.

Example: quiet   *quieter*   *quietest*

16–17 heavy   _____   _____

18–19 good   _____   _____

20–21 angry   _____   _____

Complete each sentence using a different *adverb*.

22 They screamed _____.

23 I swam _____.

24 We giggled _____.

25 He whispered _____.

Write the *plural* forms of these words.

26 roof   _____

27 circle   _____

28 lioness   _____

29 quantity   _____

30 shelf   _____

Test 2: **Spelling**

Test time: 0 — 5 — 10 minutes

Write the *contraction* for each of these.

1. have not _____
2. could have _____
3. I will _____
4. will not _____

Write each of these words correctly.

5. temprature _____
6. mischivous _____
7. ocurred _____
8. apreciate _____
9. forign _____
10. existance _____
11. familar _____
12. cemetry _____
13. aggresive _____
14. garantee _____

Add the missing double letters to each of these words.

15. a__ __idental
16. begi__ __ing
17. reco__ __end
18. courge__ __e
19. a__ __earance
20. tomo__ __ow

Add ary or ery to each of these to make a word.

21 nurs_____   25 diction_____
22 annivers_____   26 deliv_____
23 scen_____   27 imagin_____
24 burgl_____   28 gloss_____

Each of these words has a missing silent letter. Rewrite each word correctly.

29 reath   _____
30 night   _____
31 resin   _____
32 sene   _____
33 autum   _____
34 clim   _____
35 sord   _____

Add a different hyphenated prefix to each of these to make a new word.

| bi-   ex-   re-   by-   cross- |

36 weekly   _____
37 country   _____
38 colleague _____
39 election   _____
40 enter   _____

TEST 3: Comprehension

Read this extract carefully.

The Very Bloody History of Britain *by John Farman*

The Cunning Celts

[The Celts] came here [Britain] in 650 BC from central Europe apparently looking for tin – please don't ask me why! The Celts were tall, blond and blue-eyed and so got all the best girls right away. This, of course, annoyed the poor Britons even more, but there was not much they could do about it as they only had sticks and fists to fight with. The Celts set up home in the south of England around Surrey and Kent – building flash wooden forts which the poor boneheaded locals could only mill around in awe and envy.

Now England wasn't too bad a place to live for the next few hundred years (providing you were tall, blue-eyed and blond). Then in 55 BC the late Julius Caesar – star of stage and screen – arrived with a couple of legions from Rome, Italy. The refined Romans were repelled, in more ways than one by the crude Celts, who by this time had turned blue (from woad). They did, however, come back a year later with a much bigger, better-equipped army – and guess what – were repelled again.

55 BC – The Romans

You couldn't get away from the fact, however, that the Romans were much sharper than the Celts. They therefore decided that they'd infiltrate peacefully rather than invade; which was just a sneaky Italian trick. How the Celts didn't notice the daftly-dressed Roman soldiers I'll never know.

AD 43 Boadicea

This gradual infiltration took longer than expected and the Romans became rather impatient. Emperor Claudius sent another lot of legions to conquer us properly – which they did – properly! The only real trouble they encountered was a strange woman warrior from somewhere near Norwich. Her name was Boadicea and, from the only available picture I've seen, she seemed to travel everywhere in a very snazzy horse-drawn cart with blades sticking out of the wheels. This must have made parking in London rather tricky, which is probably why she burnt it to the ground. She went on to kill 70,000 Romans but, when they started getting the better of things, poisoned herself.

When In Britain Do As The Romans Do

If you can't beat a Roman, join him. Gradually the hostile Brits came round to the Roman way of thinking. The smart ones even managed to make a few lire and live Hollywood-style, in centrally heated villas covered in naff mosaics. The unsmart ones stayed in their hovels, being only serfs and slaves…. Soon everybody knew their place. Christianity was made the imperial religion and the first two centuries were to be among the most prosperous and peaceful in England's history.

Answers these questions about the extract.

1. Where did the Celts originally come from?

2. How did the Britons react when the Celts arrived?

3. When did the Romans first arrive on British soil?

4. Describe one way the Romans were different from the Celts.

5. Who was Boadicea?

6. Why was Boadicea described in the extract as 'real trouble' (line 44)?

7. What is meant by 'the hostile Brits came round to the Roman way of thinking' (lines 61–62)?

8. What is the meaning of 'prosperous' in line 70?

9. Describe what it was like in Britain during the period of Roman rule.

10. Why do you think John Farman has titled his book 'The Very Bloody History of Britain'?

Test 4: **Mixed**

Test time: 0 — 5 — 10 minutes

Add a *verb* to these sentences.

1 _____ my coat, it's raining.

2 _____, Tariq is in the next race.

3 _____, we have to get the car out the mud!

4 _____ on the carpet, Kate.

5 _____ your breakfast quickly, or you will be late.

Write the masculine version of these words.

6 daughter _____

7 cow _____

8 waitress _____

9 duck _____

10 Mrs _____

11 queen _____

Underline one *clause* in each of these sentences.

12 The children wanted to walk to school even though it was pouring with rain.

13 Jess worked hard at her story and finished it just before playtime.

14 Although the sun was hidden by the clouds the sunbathers still got burnt.

15 Tom jumped with excitement when he was invited to David's party.

16 The chicken clucked loudly after laying an egg.

Write two *antonyms* for each of these words.

17–18 hot _____   _____

19–20 hard _____   _____

21–22 love _____   _____

Write a word with the same letter string and the same pronunciation.

23 rough _____

24 dough _____

25 thorough _____

26 fought _____

Complete these words using *tial* or *cial*.

27 confiden_____

28 artifi_____

29 finan_____

30 ini_____

Test 5: Vocabulary

Test time: 0 — 5 — 10 minutes

Write these *abbreviations* in full.

1. TV _____
2. km _____
3. UK _____
4. approx. _____
5. UFO _____

Circle the words that can be used for either gender.

6–10

lioness　　teacher　　farmer

husband　　electrician　　nurse

lord　　mistress　　uncle

doctor　　niece　　headmaster

Write two *synonyms* for each word.

11–12　laugh　_____　_____

13–14　shut　_____　_____

15–16　frighten　_____　_____

17–18　drink　_____　_____

10

Write the word for the young of each of these animals.

19 pig _____

20 owl _____

21 duck _____

22 goose _____

Write a *definition* for each of these words.

23 purchase _____

24 supervise _____

25 rehearse _____

26 grumpy _____

Mix and match these words to make four *compound words*.

foot   snow   ball   man

27 _____

28 _____

29 _____

30 _____

Test 6: Mixed

Write six words using a word and a suffix from each box.

| observe | assist | confide |

| ant | ance | ent | ence |

1–6 _____ _____ _____ _____ _____ _____

Put a tick next to the words spelt correctly and a cross next to those spelt incorrectly.

7   height   _____

8   weild   _____

9   relieve   _____

10 deceive   _____

11 retreive   _____

12 cieling   _____

Write two sentences that use commas, brackets or dashes to indicate when something is in parenthesis.

13–14 _____

_____

15–16 _____

_____

Write two *onomatopoeic* words that describe the sounds that each of these make.

17–18 volcano _____ _____

19–20 plug hole _____ _____

Complete the table of *nouns*.

21–28

jealousy   herd   jacket   China
Meena   lifetime   gaggle   hate

Common nouns	Proper nouns	Collective nouns	Abstract nouns

Add an *adjectival phrase* to complete each sentence.

29 The _____ cockerel protected his chickens from the fox.

30 The washing dried quickly in the _____ _____ wind.

TEST 7: **Grammar**

Test time: 0 — 5 — 10 minutes

Change the *verbs* in each sentence into more powerful verbs.

1 The dog **ate** its food hungrily. _____

2 The children **walked** to the park. _____

3–4 Mum **said** it was time to **get** out of bed. _____ _____

5–6 As the car **drove** past, it **frightened** the lollipop lady. _____ _____

Write two *adjectives* to describe each of these *nouns*.

7–8   a _____, _____ baby

9–10   a _____, _____ car

11–12 a _____, _____ fish

13–14   _____, _____ sky

Write two examples of each of the following.

15–16   *proper noun*   _____   _____

17–18   *preposition*   _____   _____

19–20   *adverb*   _____   _____

21–22   *pronoun*   _____   _____

Use *adverbs* (for example perhaps, surely) or *modal verbs* (for example might, should) to write four sentences illustrating degrees of possibility. For example, *The shops might be open later.*

Underline the adverb or modal verb in each sentence.

23–24 _____

_____

_____

25–26 _____

_____

_____

27–28 _____

_____

_____

29–30 _____

_____

_____

TEST 8: Comprehension

Read this extract carefully.

The Ghost of Tantony Pig *by Julia Jarman*

1 *A house was being built in Hogsbottom Field, close to Laurie Gell's home.*

He strained to see in the darkness. There was definitely an animal in Hogsbottom Field, peering into the trench. Its head was down and large ears covered most of its face, but clearly visible, glistening in the moonlight was the flat edge of a moist snout.

For a moment he wondered if he ought to do something about it, tell someone. But then he thought that a pig in a pigfield or an ex-pigfield wasn't exactly an earth shattering event, wasn't a reason to call out the emergency services or even wake his mum and dad…But where had it come from, he wondered. Was it one of Arthur Ram's? Escaped from the new farm perhaps?

Now it was making its way along the bar of the H-shape, pausing every now and then to look into the trench and push with its snout.

'Yow!'

'No Gingie.'

The pig was deliberate and careful, skirting the other side of the H now, pausing from time to time to examine and push. Stop. Start. Stop. Start. Then left. Left again. Then it was turning round, to come down the other side facing him. Its head swung up and it stood still for a moment, seemed to be looking at Laurie, straight at him, its eyes tawny-gold in the moonlight.

'YOW!'

'Gingie. Wait.'

It was walking again. *Walking*. His stomach lurched. He told himself not to be stupid. Of course it was walking. That was what pigs did…And then it was running, not walking now, but rollicking towards the end of the field, where suddenly it vanished.

Vanished. That made it sound like a conjuring trick. Now you see it, now you don't. Had he really seen a pig or was it a cement mixer which looked fat and round?

Who was he kidding? He caught sight of his white knuckles gripping the window sill. The silence was heavy. He felt as if he'd been holding his breath for an impossibly long time. He opened his mouth and the air came out in a gush – and the wind began again, whipping up the soil.

Closing the window he made his way to bed. Mrs Gingerbits pushed under the covers and settled herself in the curl of his stomach. She was comfortable, like a purring hot water-bottle, but he couldn't sleep. Just lay there listening to the wind. Trembling.

…Shouts woke him. It was light. He'd slept late – and there was something wrong at the building site. A ready-mix truck had just drawn up. Laurie dressed and breakfasted quickly, hurried over the road. The driver was still yelling at Charlie Hancock.

'You ordered a ton of concrete, mate, you're getting it!'

And Charlie, very agitated, was pointing at the field. 'Where you gonna put it mate? Look at the so-called footings!'

Laurie was already looking. There was none. The site looked like a badly ploughed field…

Answers these questions about the extract.

1. How was Laurie able to see the pig in the darkness?

   _____

   _____

2. Why was Laurie surprised to see the pig where it was?

   _____

   _____

3. Why didn't Laurie wake his Mum and Dad to tell them?

   _____

   _____

4. What colour were the pig's eyes? _____

5. Copy a sentence in the extract that lets the reader know how Laurie is feeling.

   _____

6. What is 'Gingie'? _____

7. Why in line 49 is the silence described as 'heavy'?

   _____

   _____

8. Who is Charlie Hancock? _____

9. What is the significance of the final sentence in the extract?

   _____

   _____

10. Describe how you think Laurie is now feeling at the end of the extract.

    _____

    _____

Time for a break! Go to Puzzle Page 43 ▶

TEST 9: **Mixed**

Test time: 0 — 5 — 10 minutes

Underline the *conjunctions* in each sentence.

1 Thomas had a friend around for tea but Alex wasn't allowed one.

2 Kay was late for the party despite leaving home on time.

3 Bola lost his race when he tripped over his laces.

4 The dog barked and made the horse rear up.

Write a *definition* for each of these words.

5 opinion _____

6 confide _____

7 truce _____

8 incident _____

9 sudden _____

Rewrite these sentences without the *double negatives*.

10 There weren't no footballs to play with.

    _____

11 They didn't wear no school uniform on the trip.

    _____

12 There wasn't no recorder lesson today.

    _____

13 The train didn't arrive early at no platform.

    _____

Underline the correct *verb* form in each sentence.

14   The book (fell/fall) open at the page listing magic spells.

15   When it snowed Raj (sweeps/swept) the drive.

16–17 The groom (was/were) (drove/driven) to the church.

18   Hannah (found/find) her homework just in time to hand it in.

Circle the words which have a soft g.

19–24

geese   magic   legend

   register   wrong

playground   enlarge   dragon

   dungeon   disregard

mirage   ghost

Write whether these sentences are about something happening in the past, present or future.

25   I am stroking my cat.   _____

26   I will eat my tea.   _____

27   I played football.   _____

28   I made pancakes.   _____

29   I might tidy my room.   _____

30   I am exhausted.   _____

TEST 10: **Sentences**

Rewrite these sentences, adding the missing punctuation and capital letters.

1–6 did you get my e-mail gareth asked

_____

7–10 nina now she was feeling better had arranged to meet her friends

_____

_____

11–16 would you like some sweets asked deano

_____

_____

Add 'did' or 'done' to each sentence to make it correct.

17 Ivan _____ his homework as soon as he was given it.

18 "I'm sure we have _____ the right thing," confirmed Helen.

19 "_____ you know we had to bring a packed lunch today?" asked Tim.

20 They were sure they had _____ enough to win the competition.

Write these sentences as *indirect speech*.

21 "I'm glad you are coming with us, Aunty Sue," said Alex.

_____

_____

22 "We must remember our coats," Mum reminded the children.

_____

_____

Write four sentences, each with a relative clause beginning with the following words.

23 who

24 which

25 that

26 where

TEST 11: **Mixed**

Test time: 0 — 5 — 10 minutes

Underline the correct *homophone* in each bracket.

1–2 The (bough/**bow**) of the boat collided with the (bow/**bough**) of the tree.

3–4 Aimee's cut on her (heal/**heel**) didn't take long to (**heal**/heel).

5–6 The (cellar/**seller**) sold his goods from the (**cellar**/seller).

Underline the *pronouns* in the following passage.

7–11

They rushed over the rocks, desperate to get to safety before the waves came in and cut them off from the path ahead. Henry cried as he slipped and hurt his arm. It was wrapped in a jumper, as there was no time for anything else.

Underline one word in each group which is <u>not</u> a *synonym* for the rest.

12	right	decent	honest	untrue	fair
13	quiet	direct	peaceful	calm	tranquil
14	guard	protect	defend	shield	pursue
15	convey	clever	intelligent	smart	brainy
16	offend	question	quiz	ask	interrogate

Rewrite these sentences changing them from *plural* to *singular*.

17–18   The puppies raced towards the balls.

_____

19–23   They ate the ice-creams quickly as they dripped down their arms.

_____

_____

Add a *suffix* to each of these to make new words.

24   end   _____

25   help   _____

26   colour   _____

Add *tious* or *cious* to complete the words.

27   scrump_____

28   mali_____

29   flirta_____

30   fero_____

Test 12: Spelling

Test time: 0 — 5 — 10 minutes

Write the *root word* of each of these words.

1. redevelop _____
2. unanswerable _____
3. prejudge _____
4. amusement _____
5. untidy _____
6. peaceful _____
7. electrician _____
8. interconnect _____

Add able or ible to each of these to make a word.

9. excit_____
10. poss_____
11. inflat_____
12. resist_____
13. flex_____
14. divis_____
15. reli_____
16. excus_____

Each of these words has an unstressed vowel missing. Rewrite each word.

17. histry _____
18. avalable _____
19. lesure _____
20. vegtable _____
21. jewellry _____
22. diffrent _____

Test 1: Mixed (pages 2–3)

1–4 Commas are used to separate items in a list. There is a comma between each item except for the final two, which are separated by 'and' instead. Commas are also used to separate the main clause in a sentence from the additional added information.

1–2 On her way to school, Carys realised she had forgotten her glasses, swimming things, reading book and recorder. (First comma may not be included.)

3–4 Dave and Tim struggled through the rain, slipping on rocks and stumbling through the mud, as they hurried to reach cover. (Second comma may not be included.)

5 **dependable**
6 **earlier** When adding suffixes to words ending in 'y', the 'y' changes to 'i'.
7 **cordless**
8 **doubtful**
9 **likelihood** Refer to Q6.
10 **responsible** When adding suffixes to words ending in 'e', the 'e' is often removed.

11–15 Refer to definition of definitions in key words on page 47.
11 **postcode**
12 **pound, penny**
13 **portrait**
14 **prince**
15 **pudding**

16–21 Refer to definition of adjectives in key words on page 47.
16–17 **heavier, heaviest**
18–19 **better, best**
20–21 **angrier, angriest**

22–25 Refer to definition of an adverb in key words on page 47. Possible answers include:
22 *loudly*
23 *gracefully*
24 *helplessly*
25 *quietly*

26–30 Refer to definition of the plural in key words on page 47.
26 **roofs** Most singular words can be made plural by adding an 's'.
27 **circles** Refer to Q26.
28 **lionesses** If a singular word ends in 's', it can be made plural by adding 'es'.
29 **quantities** When adding suffixes to words ending in 'y'; the 'y' changes to i and 'es' is added.
30 **shelves** If a singular word ends in 'f', it can be made plural by adding 'ves'.

Test 2: Spelling (pages 4–5)

1–4 Refer to definition of a contraction in key words on page 47.
1 **haven't**
2 **could've**
3 **I'll**
4 **won't**
5 **temperature**
6 **mischievous**
7 **occurred**
8 **appreciate**
9 **foreign**
10 **existence**
11 **familiar**
12 **cemetery**
13 **aggressive**
14 **guarantee**
15 **accidental**
16 **beginning**
17 **recommend**
18 **courgette**
19 **appearance**
20 **tomorrow**

21–28 There is no set rule to identify whether a word should end in 'ary' or 'ery'.
21 **ery** nursery
22 **ary** anniversary
23 **ery** scenery
24 **ary** burglary
25 **ary** dictionary
26 **ery** delivery
27 **ary** imaginary
28 **ary** glossary
29 **w**reath
30 **k**night
31 resi**g**n
32 s**c**ene
33 autum**n**
34 clim**b**
35 s**w**ord

36–40 Refer to definition of a prefix in key words on page 47.
36 **bi-weekly**
37 **cross-country**
38 **ex-colleague**
39 **by-election**
40 **re-enter**

Test 3: Comprehension (pages 6–7)

1 **central Europe** (line 3)
2 *The Britons weren't happy about the arrival of the Celts, though were in awe of their superior skills.* (lines 7–8 and 14–15)

3 **55 BC** (line 19)
4 *The Romans were better equipped/more organised/more intelligent than the Celts.* (lines 27–34)
5 *a female Celt warrior from near Norwich who was a threat to the Romans* (lines 44–47)
6 *because she led a force that burnt down London and killed many Roman soldiers* (lines 53–54)
7 *The unhappy Brits that were invaded by the Romans eventually decided it was better to work with the Romans than against them.*
8 *successful, especially with money*
9 *It was a peaceful period in history when general living conditions improved for many* (lines 60–71)
10 *There appears to have been many 'bloody' battles to win control of Britain through different periods in history.*

Test 4: Mixed (pages 8–9)

1–5 Refer to definition of a verb in key words on page 47. Possible answers include:
1 *Grab*
2 *Watch*
3 *Push*
4 *Sit*
5 *Eat*
6 **son**
7 **bull**
8 **waiter**
9 **drake**
10 **Mr**
11 **king**
12–16 Refer to definition of a clause in key words on page 47.
12 **The children wanted to walk to school** or **even though it was pouring with rain**.
13 **Jess worked hard at her story** or **finished it just before playtime**.
14 **Although the sun was hidden by the clouds** or **the sunbathers still got burnt**.
15 **Tom jumped with excitement** or **when he was invited to David's party**.
16 **The chicken clucked loudly** or **after laying an egg**.
17–22 Refer to definition of an antonym in key words on page 47. Possible answers include:
17–18 *cold, freezing*
19–20 *soft, easy*
21–22 *hate, dislike*
23–26 The letter string 'ough' has many different pronunciations. Possible answers should rhyme, such as:

23 *tough*
24 *though*
25 *borough*
26 *thought*
27–30 In most cases, 'tial' is used if it follows a consonant, and 'cial' is used if it follows a vowel. (There are some exceptions, such as 'spatial'.)
27 **tial** confidential
28 **cial** artificial
29 **cial** financial (This is an exception to the rule.)
30 **tial** initial (This is another exception to the rule.)

Test 5: Vocabulary (pages 10–11)

1–5 Refer to the definition of abbreviations in key words on page 47.
1 **television**
2 **kilometre**
3 **United Kingdom**
4 **approximately** or **approximate**
5 **unidentified flying object**
6–10 **teacher, farmer, electrician, nurse, doctor**
11–18 Refer to definition of synonyms in key words on page 47. Possible answers include:
11–12 *giggle, chuckle*
13–14 *block, close*
15–16 *scare, terrify*
17–18 *guzzle, gulp*
19 **piglet**
20 **owlet**
21 **duckling**
22 **gosling**
23–26 Refer to definition of definitions in key words on page 47.
23 *to buy*
24 *to watch over (a task, activity or person) to make sure everything runs well*
25 *to practise*
26 *bad-tempered*
27–30 Refer to definition of compound words in key words on page 47.
27–30 **football, snowball, snowman, footman**

Test 6: Mixed (pages 12–13)

1–6 The suffixes '-ant'/'-ance' and '-ent'/'-ence' are particularly difficult to work out as they are pronounced the same and there is no definite rule to distinguish between them. If a root word can use '-ation' as a suffix, then '-ant'/'-ance' are most likely used.
1–6 **observant, observance, assistant, assistance, confident, confidence**

7–12 Although the general 'i before e except after c' rule can be applied sometimes, there are many exceptions. When the sound is ee, use 'ie' (e.g. belief); when the sound is ay, use 'ei' (e.g. neighbour). As usual, there are also some exceptions to this rule, such as caffeine.
7 ✔ This word is an exception to the rule.
8 ✗ This word follows the rule.
9 ✔ This word follows the rule.
10 ✔ This word follows the rule.
11 ✗ This word follows the rule.
12 ✗ This word follows the rule.
13–16 Refer to definition of parenthesis in key words on page 47. For example, *My brother – who has brown hair – likes playing football.*
17–20 Refer to definition of onomatopoeic words in key words on page 47. Possible answers include:
17–18 *whoosh, crackle*
19–20 *glug, drip*
21–28 Refer to definitions of nouns, common nouns, proper nouns, collective nouns and abstract nouns in key words on page 47.

Common nouns	Proper nouns	Collective nouns	Abstract nouns
jacket	China	herd	jealousy
lifetime	Meena	gaggle	hate

29–30 Refer to the definition of an adjectival phrase in key words on page 47. Possible answers include:
29 *brave, fearless and determined*
30 *strong and warm*

Test 7: Grammar (pages 14–15)

1–6 Refer to definition of verbs in key words on page 47. Possible answers include:
1 *gulped, gobbled*
2 *rushed*
3–4 *yelled; struggle, jump*
5–6 *raced; terrified*
7–14 Refer to definitions of adjectives and nouns in key words on page 47. Possible answers include:
7–8 *beautiful, happy*
9–10 *bright, shiny*
11–12 *slippery, silvery*
13–14 *grey, cloudy*
15–22 Refer to definitions of a proper noun, preposition, adverb and pronoun in key words on page 47. Possible answers include:
15–16 *Wales, Queen Elizabeth*
17–18 *in, after*
19–20 *softly, suddenly*
21–22 *she, they*

23–30 Refer to definitions of adverbs and modal verbs in key words on page 47. Four sentences, each using an adverb or modal verb to illustrate degrees of possibility, for example, *The shops should be open tonight.*

Test 8: Comprehension (pages 16–17)

1 *it glistened in the moonlight* (lines 7–8)
2 *it was wandering around a building site* (lines 1–5)
3 *it wasn't so important/it was only a pig* (lines 1–16)
4 **tawny-gold** (line 34)
5 *'His stomach lurched'* (lines 37–38); *'He caught sight of his white knuckles gripping the window sill'* (lines 47–48)
6 *his cat, Mrs Gingerbits* (lines 54–58)
7 *because it is an uncomfortable silence, loaded with worry and concern for Laurie.*
8 *the builder* (lines 66–68)
9 *It proved that Laurie had seen a pig because the land had been churned up by the pig's rooting around.*
10 *A description of how Laurie might now be feeling, e.g. frightened, worried, shocked.*

Test 9: Mixed (pages 18–19)

1–4 Refer to definition of conjunctions in key words on page 47.
1 Thomas had a friend around for tea **but** Alex wasn't allowed one.
2 Kay was late for the party **despite** leaving home on time.
3 Bola lost his race **when** he tripped over his laces.
4 The dog barked **and** made the horse rear up.
5–9 Refer to definition of definition in key words on page 47.
5 *a statement of ideas or beliefs*
6 *to trust someone with a secret*
7 *an agreement between two parties to stop fighting for a certain length of time*
8 *an event or happening*
9 *happening quickly or unexpectedly*
10–13 Refer to definition of double negatives in key words on page 47.
10 **There were no footballs to play with.** The words 'were no' may be written as 'weren't any'.
11 **They didn't wear school uniform on the trip.**
12 **There wasn't a recorder lesson today.** The words 'wasn't a' may be written as 'was no'.
13 **The train didn't arrive early at the platform.**
14–18 Refer to definition of a verb in key words on page 47.

14 The book **fell** open at the page listing magic spells.
15 When it snowed Raj **swept** the drive
16–17 The groom **was driven** to the church.
18 Hannah **found** her homework just in time to hand it in.
19–24 A 'soft g' often precedes the letters 'I', 'y' or 'e'.
19–24 **magic, legend, register, enlarge, dungeon, mirage**
25–30 Refer to definition of tense in key words on page 47.
25 present
26 future
27 past
28 past
29 future
30 present

Test 10: Sentences (pages 20–21)

1–6 "Did you get my e-mail?" Gareth asked.
7–10 Nina, now she was feeling better, had arranged to meet her friends.
11–16 "Would you like some sweets?" asked Deano.
17 Ivan **did** his homework as soon as he was given it.
18 "I'm sure we have **done** the right thing," confirmed Helen.
19 "**Did** you know we had to bring a packed lunch today?" asked Tim.
20 They were sure they had **done** enough to win the competition.
21–22 Refer to definition of indirect speech in key words on page 47.
21 *Alex said he was glad Aunty Sue was coming with them.*
22 *Mum reminded the children to remember/that they must remember their coats.*
23–26 Refer to definition of a relative clause in key words on page 47. Four sentences that include a relative clause using the listed words, for example, *That's the girl who lives near my uncle.*

Test 11: Mixed (pages 22–23)

1–6 Refer to definition of a homophone in key words on page 47.
1–2 The **bow** of the boat collided with the **bough** of the tree.
3–4 Aimee's cut on her **heel** didn't take long to **heal**.
5–6 The **seller** sold his goods from the **cellar**.
7–11 Refer to definition of a pronoun in key words on page 47.
7–11 **They** rushed over the rocks, desperate to get to safety before the waves came in and cut **them** off from the path ahead. Henry cried as **he** slipped and hurt his arm. **It** was wrapped in a jumper, as there was no time for **anything** else.
12–16 Refer to definition of a synonym in key words on page 47.
12 untrue
13 direct
14 pursue
15 convey
16 offend
17–23 Refer to definitions of the plural and the singular in key words on page 47.
17–18 **The puppy raced towards the ball.**
19–23 **She/He ate the ice-cream quickly as it dripped down her/his arm.**
24–26 Refer to definition of a suffix in key words on page 47. Possible answers include:
24 endless, ending
25 helpful, helper, helping
26 colourless, colourful
27–30 The suffix '-tious' is usually used when the root word can also have a '-tion' ending. If the root word ends in '-ce', the suffix '-cious' is usually used (of course, there are exceptions).
27 **tious** scrumptious
28 **cious** malicious The root word is malice.
29 **tious** flirtatious The word flirtation can also be made from the root word.
30 **cious** ferocious The root word is fierce.

Test 12: Spelling (pages 24–25)

1–8 Refer to definition of a root word in key words on page 47.
1 develop
2 answer
3 judge
4 amuse
5 tidy
6 peace
7 electric
8 connect
9–16 If the root word is recognisable as a whole (or almost whole) word, then generally the suffix is -able.
9 **able** excitable The root word is excite.
10 **ible** possible
11 **able** inflatable The root word is inflate.
12 **ible** resistible The root word is resist, but this is an exception to the rule.
13 **ible** flexible
14 **ible** divisible
15 **able** reliable The root word is rely.

16 **able** excusable The root word is excuse.
17–22 Unstressed vowels are vowels (a, e, i, o, u) that aren't easy to hear in a word.
17 **history**
18 **available**
19 **leisure**
20 **vegetable**
21 **jewellery**
22 **different**
23–28 *There* refers to a place; *their* shows belonging to someone; *they're* is a contraction of *they are*.
23 **They're** They're going to be late.
24 **there** We must be nearly there by now!
25 **their** We'll collect their sleeping bags on the way home.
26 **There** There seems to be a problem with the car.
27–28 **They're, their** They're great friends but they argue about their favourite football teams all the time!
29–34 Refer to Test 6 Mixed Q7–12.
29 **veil**
30 **height** This is an exception to the rule.
31 **foreign** This is an exception to the rule.
32 **cashier**
33 **relief**
34 **receipt**
35 **flatter** For one-syllable words, double the final consonant when adding a suffix.
36 **preferring** In '-fer' root word endings, when the second syllable is stressed (once the suffix has been added), the last 'r' is doubled. When the first syllable is stressed, the root word spelling remains the same.
37 **busier** For words ending in 'y', adding a suffix often changes the 'y' to 'i'.
38 **transferred** Refer to Q36.
39 **referred** Refer to Q36.
40 **relieved** For words ending in 'f', adding a suffix sometimes changes the 'f' to 'v'.

Test 13: Comprehension (pages 26–27)

1 *we don't know; it was written anonymously* (line 55)
2 *they sang* (lines 4–5)
3 *she wanted to wear something more practical outside* (lines 7–11)
4 **milk-white** (or just white – line 19)
5 *caught sight of*
6 *she wanted a freer, or more exciting, life* (lines 35–37)
7 *upset and surprised – he wanted to try to persuade her to come back home* (lines 40–45)
8 *messy, dirty, unclean, untidy*
9 *the language, the description of the servants, horse, home, etc.*
10 *happy, relieved and free to have left the home where she obviously felt unhappy*

Test 14: Mixed (pages 28–29)

1 **pizza – Italy**
2 **boomerang – Australia**
3 **restaurant – France**
4 **pyjamas – India**
5 **adverb**
6 **verb**
7 **preposition**
8 **abstract noun/noun/verb**
9 **pronoun**
10 **adjective/verb**
11–14 Refer to definition of indirect speech in key words on page 47.
11 *Chloe asked if they could go swimming.*
12 *The Bayliss family complained that they always had fish fingers for tea.*
13 *Dad suggested they drive past Buckingham Palace.*
14 *Elizabeth laughed, saying she loved pony riding./Elizabeth laughed that she loved pony riding.*
15–19 Refer to definition of a prefix in key words on page 47.
15 **mis** misquote
16 **mis** mishandle
17 **dis** dismount
18 **dis** dislodge
19 **mis** misspell
20–30 "I feel so tired," complained Jim. "That's because it is one o'clock in the morning!" said the babysitter.

Test 15: Vocabulary (pages 30–31)

1–5 Refer to definition of a definition in key words on page 47.
1 **impossibility**
2 **irritable**
3 **island**
4 **ivy**
5 **investigate**
6–10 Refer to definition of the alphabetical order in key words on page 47.
6 **smart**
7 **smirk**
8 **smoke**
9 **smother**
10 **smuggle**
11–14 Possible answers include: google, frisbee, laptop and smartphone.

15–18 Refer to definition of onomatopoeic in key words on page 47.
15 *heehaw*
16 *roar*
17 *honk*
18 *cluck*
19–26 Refer to definition of antonyms in key words on page 47. Possible answers include:
19–20 *untidy, messy*
21–22 *sad, unhappy*
23–24 *weak, feeble*
25–26 *damp, wet*
27 *cloud*
28 *cats*
29 *fence*
30 *music*

Test 16: Mixed (pages 32–33)

1–6 Refer to definition of abbreviations in key words on page 47.
1 **HRH**
2 **DIY**
3 **Dec**
4 **PM**
5 **OAP**
6 **PO**
7–12 'to' is a preposition; 'too' is an adverb meaning both 'overly' or 'excessively' (e.g. it's too loud) and 'also' (e.g. I'm going too); 'two' is a number.
7 **too** The chips were too hot.
8 **Too** Too many people were trying to get on the bus.
9–10 **to, to** Danielle wanted to go to Rupa's party.
11 **two** The two boys ran as fast as they could.
12 **to** The teacher spoke sternly to the giggling children.
13–16 "Time for your piano lesson," Mum called. OR "Time for your piano lesson!" Mum called.
17–20 "Where have you put my phone?" asked Rebecca.
21–24 Refer to definitions of an adjective and a noun in key words on page 47. Possible answers include:
21 *sparkly, glamorous*
22 *terrified, prickly*
23 *mad, strict*
24 *empty, bustling*
25–27 Refer to definitions of conjunctions in key words on page 47. Possible answers include:
25 *The rain poured but they still had a BBQ.*
26 *There was a fire in the school hall although it didn't do much damage.*
27 *Jake threw the ball and it landed in someone's garden.*

28–30 Refer to definitions of an antonym in key words on page 47. Possible answers include:
28 *disrespect*
29 *daft*
30 *whisper*

Test 17: Grammar (pages 34–35)

1–8 Refer to definitions of nouns, common nouns, proper nouns, collective nouns and abstract nouns in key words on page 47.

Common nouns	Proper nouns	Collective nouns	Abstract nouns
insects	Jake	swarms	dislike
pets	Tyrone	colonies	fear

9–13 Refer to definitions of an adjectival phrase and nouns in key words on page 47. Possible answers include:
9 *the old and musty book*
10 *the long, hot and busy summer*
11 *the fearless and amazing acrobat*
12 *the beautiful and interesting country of India*
13 *a lovely, old family photograph*
14–18 Refer to definitions of a conjunction in key words on page 47. Possible answers include:
14 *because*
15 *although*
16 *but*
17 *as*
18 *so*
19–24 Refer to definitions of adverbs and prepositions in key words on page 47.
19–20 Everyone watched (anxiously) as the rope was lowered over the edge of the cliff.
21–22 The children wandered off (gloomily) despite being given some money to spend.
23–24 Nazar worked (happily) knowing as soon as he'd finished cleaning the car he could go inside to watch the rugby match.
25–30 Refer to definition of possessive pronouns in key words on page 47.
25–30 Three sentences, each sentence containing two possessive pronouns, e.g. *Ours is bigger than theirs.*

Test 18: Comprehension (pages 36–37)

1 **Nairobi** (line 5)
2 *dirt instead of paved roads; background noise of cockerels and cows instead of car horns and radios* (lines 7–11)
3 *the daughter of Boniface and Pauline Kamau* (line 20)

4 *one's native language/the language a person first learns to speak*
5 *Many of the plants grown in Murang'a differ to those grown here because of the different climate.*
6 *Pauline felt comfortable back home with her parents and possibly liked getting away from the busy city.* (lines 28–29, 40–45)
7–8 *Joyce and Sharon's grandparents must get their water from a stream and grow their own food. Most grandparents in England get their water from taps in their house and buy food in shops.*
9 *If they moved back to the country, getting a job to earn enough money to take care of the young family would be much harder than it is in the city.*
10 *Child's own answers, such as the watching of TV, enjoying time with cousins, staying with grandparents etc.*

Test 19: Mixed (pages 38–39)

1–5 Refer to definition of a synonym in key words on page 47. Possible answers include:
1 *section*
2 *unoccupied*
3 *selfish, mean*
4 *obvious*
5 *recall*
6–11 Refer to Test 1 Mixed Q26–30.
6 **torches**
7 **princesses**
8 **thieves**
9 **bikes**
10 **valleys**
11 **suffixes**
12–16 Refer to definition of a preposition in key words on page 47.
12 **under**
13 **at**
14 **with**
15 **above**
16 **on**
17–20 Refer to definitions of verbs and suffix in key words on page 47. When adding a suffix, if the root word ends in 'e', it usually gets removed.
17 **dramatise**
18 **solidify**
19 **thicken**
20 **fertilise**

21–25 An apostrophe is used to show a missing letter where two words have become a contraction.
21 **You'll** (You will)
22 **mustn't** (must not)
23 **Let's** (Let us)
24 **could've** (could have)
25 **I'd** (I had)
26 *though*
27 *weight*
28 *grown*
29 *hour*
30 *door*

Test 20: Sentences (pages 40–41)

1–4 Commas are used to separate items in a list. There is a comma between each item except for the final two, which are separated by 'and' instead. Commas are also used to separate the main clause in a sentence from the additional added information.
1–4 Two sentences, each with two correctly marked commas, e.g. *Katy put her pencil, pen, ruler and sharpener in her backpack.*
5–9 Questions usually begin with a question word and require a response. Statements generally contain a subject, verb and object. If a question begins with a verb followed by the subject (*Are you hungry?*), it can usually be converted to a statement by swapping the subject and verb (*You are hungry*).
5 **It is time to meet in the park.**
6 **We are going on holiday to Devon.**
7 **Liverpool won/did win the Premiership.**
8 **The school is closed because of the snow that fell last night.**
9 **The cows are milked twice a day.**
10–15 'is' is used with a singular noun; 'are' is used with a plural noun.
10 **are**
11 **are**
12 **is**
13 **is**
14 **Is**
15 **are**
16–28 "What time does the film start?" asked Brenna. She was worried they wouldn't have time to buy popcorn before it started.
"We have plenty of time," her dad reassured her.

Puzzle 1 (page 42)

sausage – usage, age, sage, us, sag, a
wardrobe – ward, robe, rob, war, be, a
mathematics – math, at, the, he, them, mat, hem, tic, tics, thematic, thematics, a
scarecrow – scar, scare, car, row, are, crow, care, a
coincidentally – coincide, coincidental, dent, dental, tall, den, ally, all, incident, incidental, incidentally, tally, in, coin, a

Puzzle 2 (page 43)

An adjective beginning with each letter of the alphabet – 'x' will be the biggest challenge and a dictionary could be used to help with this one!

Puzzle 3 (page 44)

Child's own answers to a number of word problems e.g.
marmalade *maroon marry mask mass master match material maths matter mattress maximum mayor meadow mean measles*
measure
A word with all vowels = *aeronautics*

Puzzle 4 (page 45)

north = thorn
parties = pirates, traipse
vowels = wolves
team = meat, mate, tame
eighth = height
thicken = kitchen
Three anagrams chosen by your child

Puzzle 5 (page 46)

silly – **sensible**
official – **unofficial**
dissatisfied – **happy**
huge – **tiny**
incorrect – **right**
unclear – **legible**
smooth – **rough**

Write there, their or they're in each gap.

23 _____ going to be late.

24 We must be nearly _____ by now!

25 We'll collect _____ sleeping bags on the way home.

26 _____ seems to be a problem with that car.

27–28 _____ great friends but they argue about _____ favourite football teams all the time!

Add ie or ei to each of these to make a word.

29 v__ __l

30 h__ __ght

31 for__ __gn

32 cash__ __r

33 rel__ __f

34 rec__ __pt

Complete these word sums. Watch out for the spelling changes!

35 flat + er = _____

36 prefer + ing = _____

37 busy + er = _____

38 transfer + ed = _____

39 refer + ed = _____

40 relief + ed = _____

Time for a break! Go to Puzzle Page 44

Test 13: Comprehension

Read this poem carefully.

The Wraggle Taggle Gypsies

1   There were three gypsies a-come to my door,
    And down-stairs ran this lady, O!
    One sang high, and another sang low,
5   And the other sang, Bonny, bonny,
    Biscay, O!

    Then she pulled off her silk finished gown
    And put on hose of leather, O!
10 The ragged, ragged rags about our door –
    She's gone with the wraggle taggle gypsies, O!

    It was late last night, when my lord came home,
15 Enquiring for his a-lady, O!
    The servants said on every hand:
    'She's gone with the wraggle taggle gypsies, O!'

    'O saddle to me my milk-white steed,
20 Go and fetch me my pony, O!
    That I may ride and seek my bride,
    Who is gone with the wraggle taggle gypsies, O!'

    O he rode high and he rode low,
25 He rode through woods and copses too,
    Until he came to an open field,
    And there he espied his a-lady, O!

    'What makes you leave your house and land?
30 What makes you leave your money, O!
    What makes you leave your new-wedded lord;
    To go with the wraggle taggle gypsies, O!'

35 'What care I for my house and my land?
    What care I for my money, O?
    What care I for my new-wedded lord?
    I'm off with the wraggle taggle gypsies, O!'

40 'Last night you slept on a goose-feather bed,
    With the sheet turned down so bravely, O!
    And to-night you'll sleep in a cold open
45 field,
    Along with the wraggle taggle gypsies, O!'

    'What care I for a goose-feather bed,
    With the sheet turned down so bravely,
50 O!
    For to-night I shall sleep in a cold open field,
    Along with the wraggle taggle gypsies, O!'

Anon.

Answer these questions about the poem.

1. Who wrote this poem? _____

2. What did the gypsies do at the lady's door?
   _____

3. Why do you think the lady took off her silk gown?
   _____

4. What colour was the lord's horse?
   _____

5. What does the word 'espied' (line 27) mean?
   _____

6. Why did the lady leave with the gypsies?
   _____
   _____

7. Describe how the lord felt about his wife leaving.
   _____
   _____

8. What impression does the phrase 'wraggle, taggle' give you about the gypsies?
   _____

9. How do we know this poem was not written in the present day?
   _____

10. At the end of the poem, how do you think the lady is feeling? Why?
    _____
    _____

Test 14: **Mixed**

Test time: 0 — 5 — 10 minutes

Draw lines to link each word with the country from which it is borrowed.

1. pizza — Australia
2. boomerang — India
3. restaurant — Italy
4. pyjamas — France

Which part of speech is each of these words?

5. beautifully _____
6. wrote _____
7. behind _____
8. love _____
9. they _____
10. blunt _____

Change these sentences into *indirect speech*.

11. "Can we go swimming?" Chloe asked.
    _____

12. "We always have fish fingers for tea," complained the Bayliss family.
    _____

13. "Let's drive past Buckingham Palace," suggested Dad.
    _____

14. "I love pony riding!" laughed Elizabeth.
    _____

28

Select the *prefix* mis or dis for each of these words.

15 _____quote

16 _____handle

17 _____mount

18 _____lodge

19 _____spell

Rewrite the following correctly.

20–30   i feel so tired complained jim that's because it is one o'clock in the morning said the babysitter

_____

_____

_____

_____

_____

Test 15: Vocabulary

Write one word for each *definition*. Each word begins with the letter i.

1 Something that cannot be done under any circumstances. _____

2 Grumpy and easily annoyed. _____

3 A piece of land surrounded by water. _____

4 A leafy, evergreen plant that can climb up walls. _____

5 To look into something or someone. _____

Write these words in *alphabetical order*.

smirk   smother   smart   smuggle   smoke

6 _____

7 _____

8 _____

9 _____

10 _____

Write four words that have been invented in the last 100 years.

11 _____

12 _____

13 _____

14 _____

Write an *onomatopoeic* word for the sound that each of these animals makes.

15 donkey _____

16 lion _____

17 goose _____

18 hen _____

Write two *antonyms* for each of these words.

19–20 tidy _____   _____

21–22 happy _____   _____

23–24 strong _____   _____

25–26 dry _____   _____

Choose a word to complete each expression.

fence   cloud   music   cats

27 Every _____ has a silver lining.

28 It is raining _____ and dogs.

29 To sit on the _____.

30 To face the _____.

TEST 16: **Mixed**

Test time: 0 — 5 — 10 minutes

Write the *abbreviations* of these words.

1. His Royal Highness _____
2. do it yourself _____
3. December _____
4. Prime Minister _____
5. old age pensioner _____
6. Post Office _____

Add 'to', 'too' or 'two' to each sentence to make it correct.

7. The chips were _____ hot.
8. _____ many people were trying to get on the bus.
9–10. Danielle wanted _____ go _____ Rupa's party.
11. The _____ boys ran as fast as they could.
12. The teacher spoke sternly _____ the giggling children.

Rewrite these sentences with the missing punctuation.

13–16. Time for your piano lesson Mum called

_____

_____

17–20. Where have you put my phone asked Rebecca

_____

_____

32

Add an interesting *adjective* to describe each of these *nouns*.

21   the _____ dress

22   the _____ hedgehog

23   the _____ professor

24   the _____ restaurant

Use *conjunctions* to write each of these pairs of short sentences as one sentence.

25   The rain poured. They still had a BBQ.

   _____

26   There was a fire in the school hall. It didn't do much damage.

   _____

   _____

27   Jake threw the ball. It landed in someone's garden.

   _____

Write an *antonym* for each of these words.

28   respect   _____

29   clever   _____

30   scream   _____

TEST 17: **Grammar**

Test time: 0 — 5 — 10 minutes

Complete the table using some of the *nouns* in the short passage.

1–8 Jake had a dislike of insects. He worried that swarms or colonies might attack him! Tyrone wanted to help him get over his fear and so told him to think of them as pets!

Common nouns	Proper nouns	Collective nouns	Abstract nouns

Write an *adjectival phrase* about each of these *nouns*.

9   a book

_____

10   the summer

_____

11   an acrobat

_____

12   India

_____

13   a photograph

_____

Complete each sentence by adding a different *conjunction*.

14   Faye couldn't go to the party _____ she was unwell.

15   The flowers opened in the sun _____ there was a cold wind blowing.

16   Annie was painting in the kitchen _____ the cat had taken cover under the table!

17   Gareth was terrified _____ the spider made its way towards him.

18   They missed their train _____ they had to catch a bus.

34

Circle the *adverbs* and underline the *prepositions* in these sentences.

19–20   Everyone watched anxiously as the rope was lowered over the edge of the cliff.

21–22   The children wandered off gloomily despite being given some money to spend.

23–24   Nazar worked happily knowing as soon as he'd finished cleaning the car he could go inside to watch the rugby match.

Write three sentences, each including two *possessive pronouns*.

25–26   _____

_____

27–28   _____

_____

29–30   _____

_____

TEST 18: Comprehension

Read this article carefully.

The Kamaus from Kenya
by Xan Rice

1 For the half-term holidays, the Kamaus went upcountry to the farming village where Pauline's parents live. Though just 60 miles from the Kenyan capital, Nairobi, Murang'a is a very different world.

Tarred road gives way to dirt; concrete urban sprawl to rich red soil. The background noise comes from cockerels and cows rather than the car hooters and blaring radios of the big city.

The children love visiting their grandparents. Though Joyce is something of a TV addict, she and Sharon revel in the wide-open space and the chance to play all day with their cousins, who seldom make it to Nairobi.

They also practise speaking Kikuyu, which should be their mother tongue. Boniface and Pauline are native Kikuyu speakers, but at home in Nairobi they communicate in Kiswahili, which together with English is Kenya's official national language and predominates in the urban areas. At school, Joyce learns only the two national languages, and her Kikuyu is rusty at best....

Pauline also enjoys being home with her parents. As their first-born child, she assumes the greatest responsibility of all her siblings for her parents' well-being. For now they are doing just fine.

On a hectare of land, they grow maize, beans, bananas, sugarcane, sweet potatoes, avocados and coffee. They also have a cow, a few goats, chickens and rabbits. Some of the produce is eaten; the rest taken to the wholesale market.

Pauline quickly slipped back into the lifestyle of her youth. She fetched water from the nearby stream. She worked in the fields. In the evenings, she helped prepare dinner. It made her nostalgic, and after the holiday Pauline told Boniface that they should think of moving to the countryside.

But Boniface was not tempted. Murang'a in particular, just a few miles from where he was raised, holds too many memories of a difficult childhood. Then there is the issue of work. Being a taxi-driver in Nairobi is a tough job, but at least it provides a steady income – far more than he could ever make as a small-scale farmer.

Article from the Guardian *by Xan Rice*

Answer these questions about the article.

1. Where do the Kamaus live in Kenya?
   _____

2. List two differences between life in Murang'a and life in Nairobi.
   _____
   _____

3. Who is Joyce?
   _____

4. What is a 'mother tongue' (line 19)?
   _____

5. What do you notice about the foods grown in Murang'a compared to in England?
   _____

6. Why do you think Pauline wanted to move back to the countryside?
   _____

7–8. Describe two ways the life of these children's grandparents differs from the lives of the grandparents of many children in the United Kingdom.
   _____
   _____
   _____
   _____

9. What is meant by the sentence 'Then there is the issue of work' (lines 51–52)?
   _____
   _____

10. How many similarities can you list between your family and the Kamau family?
    _____
    _____

37 Total

Test 19: **Mixed**

Test time: 0 — 5 — 10 minutes

Write a *synonym* for each of the words in bold.

1 Please pass me the **part** of the newspaper that is for children.

   _____

2 The bungalow in our street has been **vacant** for a year. _____

3 She is so **stingy**, she never shares her colouring pens. _____

4 It was **clear** from his pale face that he had hurt his ankle badly.

   _____

5 Gemma, can you **remember** what I asked you to do next?

   _____

Write the *plural* forms of these words.

6 torch   _____   9 bike   _____

7 princess   _____   10 valley   _____

8 thief   _____   11 suffix   _____

Circle the *preposition* in each of these sentences.

12 George's shoes were hidden under the sofa.

13 Tea will be ready at six-thirty.

14 Helen mended her broken tyre with a puncture repair kit.

15 The river flooded above the height of the fence posts.

16 The dog slept soundly on his owner's bed!

Change these words into *verbs* by adding a *suffix*.

en   ise   ify

17 drama _____

18 solid _____

19 thick _____

20 fertile _____

Add the missing apostrophes.

21 Youll have to learn your spellings for the test!

22 We mustnt be late.

23 Lets buy some sweets, please.

24 You couldve stayed longer.

25 I wish Id brought my bike to ride.

Write a word with the same letter string as underlined in each of these words, but a different pronunciation.

26 t<u>ough</u> _____

27 h<u>ei</u>ght _____

28 br<u>ow</u>n _____

29 f<u>ou</u>r _____

30 sp<u>oo</u>n _____

Test 20: Sentences

Test time: 0 — 5 — 10 minutes

Write two sentences. Each sentence needs to have two commas.

1–2 _____

_____

3–4 _____

_____

Write these questions as statements.

5 Is it time to meet in the park?

_____

6 Are we going on holiday to Devon?

_____

7 Did Liverpool win the Premiership?

_____

8 Is the school closed because of the snow that fell last night?

_____

9 Are the cows milked twice a day?

_____

40

Add 'is' or 'are' to each sentence to make it correct.

10 On Saturday, Kellie and Sarah _____ coming for a sleepover.

11 We _____ still waiting for the train!

12 Hussan _____ working hard to improve his skateboarding.

13 Daniel _____ going to walk the dog when he gets home.

14 _____ Sam's answer right?

15 Where _____ your gloves?

Rewrite this short passage correctly.

16–28

what time does the film start asked brenna

she was worried they wouldn't have time to buy popcorn before it started

we have plenty of time her dad reassured her

_____

_____

_____

_____

_____

_____

_____

Puzzle 1

Each of these words has within it a number of smaller words.
How many smaller words can you find in each word, without rearranging the letters or missing letters out?

sausage

_____

wardrobe

_____

mathematics

_____

scarecrow

_____

coincidentally

_____

Find your own word that has at least five smaller words within it.
Try it out on someone.

_____

Puzzle ❷

Can you find 26 different *adjectives*, each beginning with a different letter of the alphabet?

a _____   b _____   c _____

d _____   e _____   f _____

g _____   h _____   i _____

j _____   k _____   l _____

m _____   n _____   o _____

p _____   q _____   r _____

s _____   t _____   u _____

v _____   w _____   x _____

y _____   z _____

Circle the five most imaginative *adjectives* you have written.

Puzzle 3

Answer these problems, then try again using a dictionary!

List as many words as you can that lie alphabetically between the words 'marmalade' and 'measure'.

My unaided answers

My answers with the help of a dictionary

Write the longest word you can think of.

_____

Write the longest word you can find in a dictionary.

_____

Write a word with as many vowels as possible.

_____

Write a word from the dictionary that uses as many vowels as possible.

_____

Can you find a word in the dictionary that uses all of the vowel letters?

_____

Puzzle 4

Look carefully at these words.

spoon   **sister**   **petal**

If the letters in each word are rearranged they will make a new word. These words are called anagrams.

spoon	=	**snoop**
sister	=	**resist**
petal	=	**plate**

Your challenge is to find the hidden words by rearranging the letters in these words, as quickly as possible!

north   _____

parties   _____

vowels   _____

team   _____

eighth   _____

thicken   _____

Now make three anagrams of your own.

_____ = _____

_____ = _____

_____ = _____

Puzzle 5

g	f	r	a	t	u	h	m	c	i
s	e	n	s	i	b	l	e	t	p
d	w	e	m	n	s	q	h	o	p
v	h	q	c	y	n	g	c	r	e
t	e	a	k	d	i	y	a	o	g
i	e	j	p	r	k	r	d	u	i
t	w	g	j	p	o	d	s	g	b
e	l	s	i	a	y	n	e	h	y
u	n	o	f	f	i	c	i	a	l
p	i	t	l	e	g	i	b	l	e

Look in the wordsearch to find *antonyms* for the following words.
Write the words you have found.

silly   _____

official   _____

dissatisfied   _____

huge   _____

incorrect   _____

unclear   _____

smooth   _____

Key words

Some special words are used in this book. You will find them picked out in *italics*. These words are explained here.

abbreviation	a word that has been shortened
abstract noun	a noun referring to a concept or idea, for example love, beauty
adjectival phrase	a group of words describing a noun
adjective	a word that describes somebody or something
adverb	a word that gives extra meaning to a verb
alphabetical order	words arranged in the order of the letters in the alphabet
antonym	a word with a meaning opposite to another word, for example hot/cold
clause	a section of a sentence with a verb
collective noun	a word referring to a group or collection of things, for example a swarm of bees
common noun	a general name of a person, place or thing, for example boy, office
compound word	a word made up of two other words, for example football
conjunction	a word used to link sentences, phrases or words, for example and, but
contraction	two words shortened into one with an apostrophe placed where the letter/s have been dropped, for example do not/don't
definition	the meaning of a word
double negative	two negative words in a sentence that make the idea in the sentence positive, for example I am *not* going to buy *no* bike (which means I am going to buy a bike)
homophone	a word that has the same sound as another but a different meaning or spelling, for example right/write
indirect speech	what has been said without using the exact words or inverted commas
modal verb	a verb that changes the meaning of other verbs, for example can, will
noun	a naming word
onomatopoeic	a word that echoes a sound, associated with its meaning, for example hiss
parenthesis	this is a word or phrase that is separated off from the main sentence by brackets, commas or dashes usually because it contains additional information not essential to its understanding
phrase	a group of words that do not contain both a subject and a verb
plural	more than one, for example cats
possessive pronoun	a pronoun showing to whom something belongs, for example mine, ours
prefix	a group of letters added to the beginning of a word, for example un, dis
preposition	a word that links nouns and pronouns to other parts of a sentence, for example he sat *behind* the door
pronoun	a word that can be used instead of a noun
proper noun	the specific name or title of a person or a place, for example Ben, London
relative clause	a special type of clause that makes the meaning of a noun more specific, for example The prize *that I won* was a book
root word	a word to which a prefix or suffix can be added to make another word, for example quick – *quickly*
singular	one of something, for example cat
suffix	a group of letters added to the end of a word, for example ly, ful
synonym	a word with a very similar meaning to another word, for example quick/fast
tense	tells when an action was done, for example past (*I slept*), present (*I am sleeping*).
verb	a 'doing' or 'being' word

Progress Grid

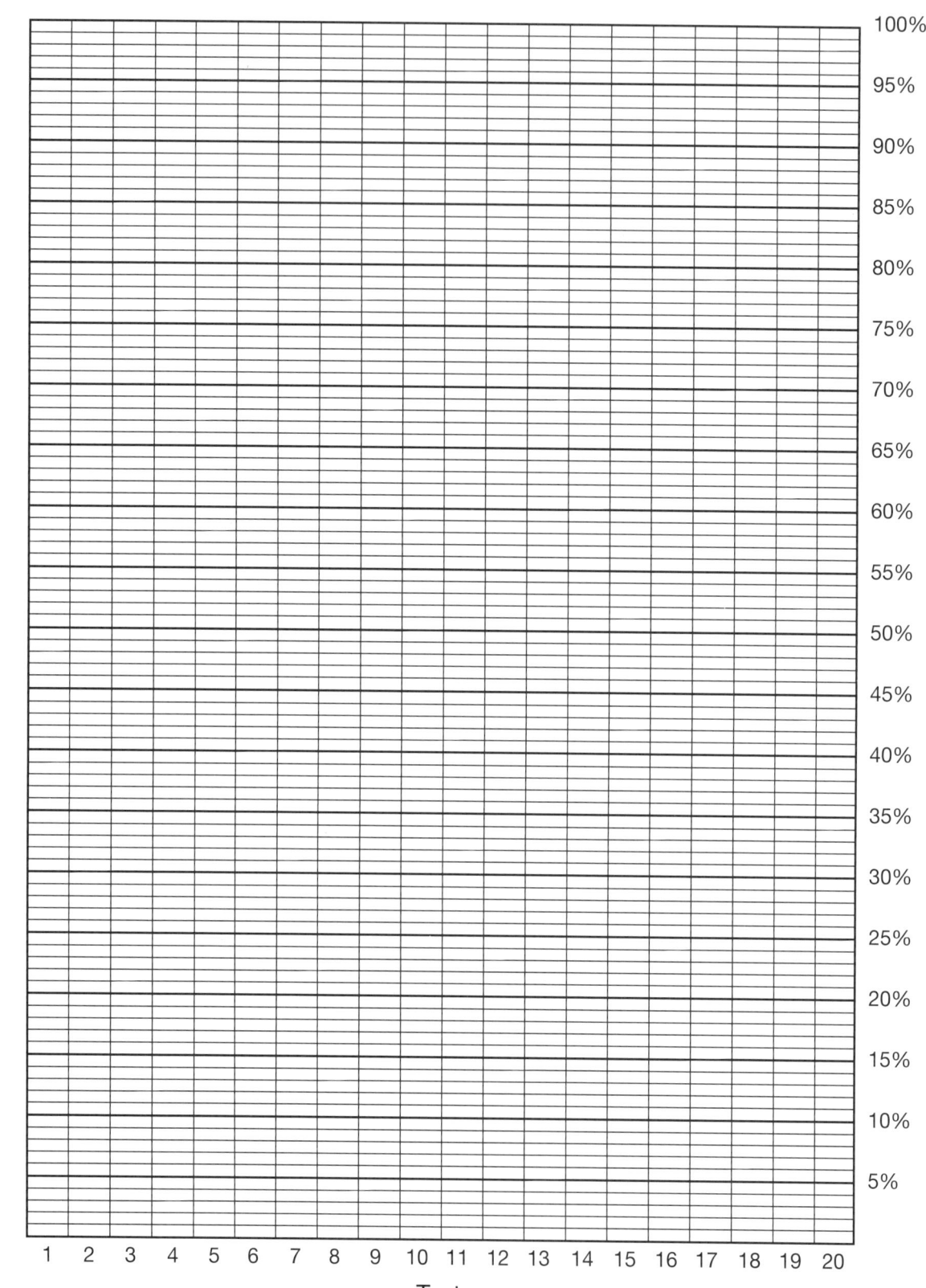